LOOK INSIDE
CROSS-SECTIONS
TRAINS

LOOK INSIDE
CROSS-SECTIONS
TRAINS

WRITTEN BY
MICHAEL JOHNSTONE

DORLING KINDERSLEY
LONDON • NEW YORK • STUTTGART

A DORLING KINDERSLEY BOOK

Art Editor Dorian Spencer Davies
Designer Sharon Grant, Sara Hill
Senior Art Editor C. David Gillingwater
Project Editor Constance Novis
Senior Editor John C. Miles
U.S. Editor Camela Decaire
Production Louise Barratt

First American edition, 1995
2 4 6 8 10 9 7 5 3 1
Published in the United States
by Dorling Kindersley Publishing, Inc.,
95 Madison Avenue, New York, New York 10016

Library of Congress Cataloging - in - Publication Data

Johnstone, Michael.
Trains / by Michael Johnstone: illustrated by Richard Chasemore
...[et al.] – – 1st American ed.
p. cm. – (Look inside cross-sections)
Includes index.
ISBN 0-7894-0319-6
1. Railroads – – Juvenile literature.
[1. Railroads – – Trains.]
I. Chasemore, Richard, ill.
II. Title. III. Series.
TF148.J66 1995
625. 1 – – dc20   95 – 15135
                                    CIP
                                    AC

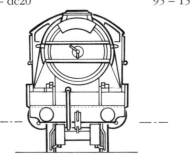

Reproduced by Dot Gradations, Essex
Printed and bound by Proost, Belgium

CONTENTS

ROCKET 6-7

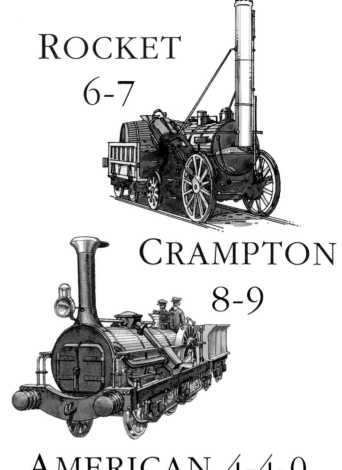

CRAMPTON 8-9

AMERICAN 4-4-0 10-11

STIRLING "SINGLE" 12-13

TANK ENGINE
14-15

HEAVY FREIGHT
16-17 / 18-19

PACIFIC
20-21

RACK LOCO
22-23

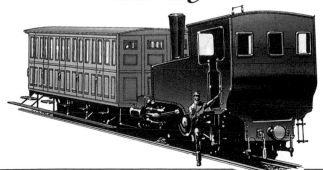

ELECTRO-DIESEL
24-25

LE SHUTTLE
26-27

TIMELINE
28-29

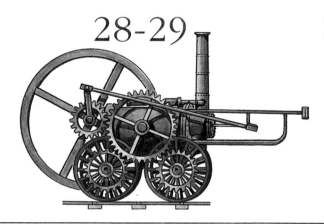

GLOSSARY
30-31

INDEX
32

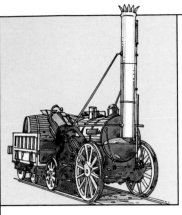

ROCKET

Tʜᴏᴜsᴀɴᴅs ᴏғ ʏᴇᴀʀs ᴀɢᴏ, ᴛʜᴇ ᴀɴᴄɪᴇɴᴛ Gʀᴇᴇᴋs ᴍᴀᴅᴇ ɢʀᴏᴏᴠᴇs in stone paths to guide wagon wheels. In the sixteenth century people first laid wooden tracks when they realized that carts ran more easily along rails than on rough ground. By the eighteenth century, England had a network of horse-drawn railroads. But by the nineteenth century, inventors were exploring the possibility of using steam locomotives rather than horses for pulling power. Businessmen wanted a cheaper alternative to horses, and steam was the answer.

The competition
In 1829, a group of businessmen decided to build a railroad between Manchester and Liverpool. They couldn't make up their minds whether to use horse-drawn carriages or cars pulled by a steam locomotive. They announced a competition for anyone who could produce a reliable steam engine. Robert Stephenson built and entered the Rocket, which won the trial hands down.

Hot stuff
The Rocket and other steam engines had a firebox in which coal was burned to boil water and produce steam. In the Rocket, hot gases from the fire passed along tubes through the water in the boiler. Steam rose into a dome and then went along the main pipes to the cylinders.

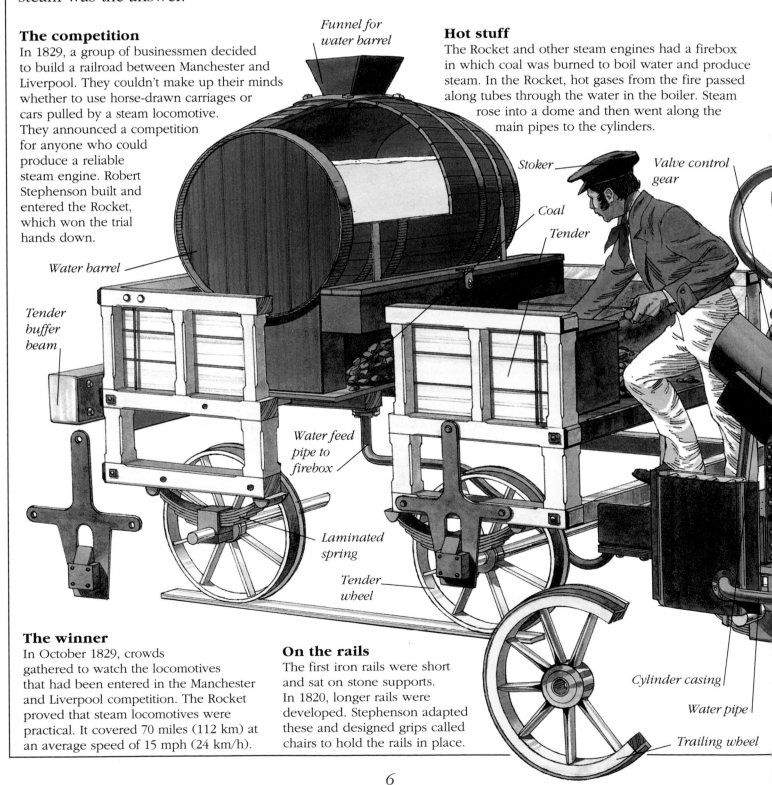

Funnel for water barrel

Stoker

Valve control gear

Coal

Tender

Water barrel

Tender buffer beam

Water feed pipe to firebox

Laminated spring

Tender wheel

Cylinder casing

Water pipe

Trailing wheel

The winner
In October 1829, crowds gathered to watch the locomotives that had been entered in the Manchester and Liverpool competition. The Rocket proved that steam locomotives were practical. It covered 70 miles (112 km) at an average speed of 15 mph (24 km/h).

On the rails
The first iron rails were short and sat on stone supports. In 1820, longer rails were developed. Stephenson adapted these and designed grips called chairs to hold the rails in place.

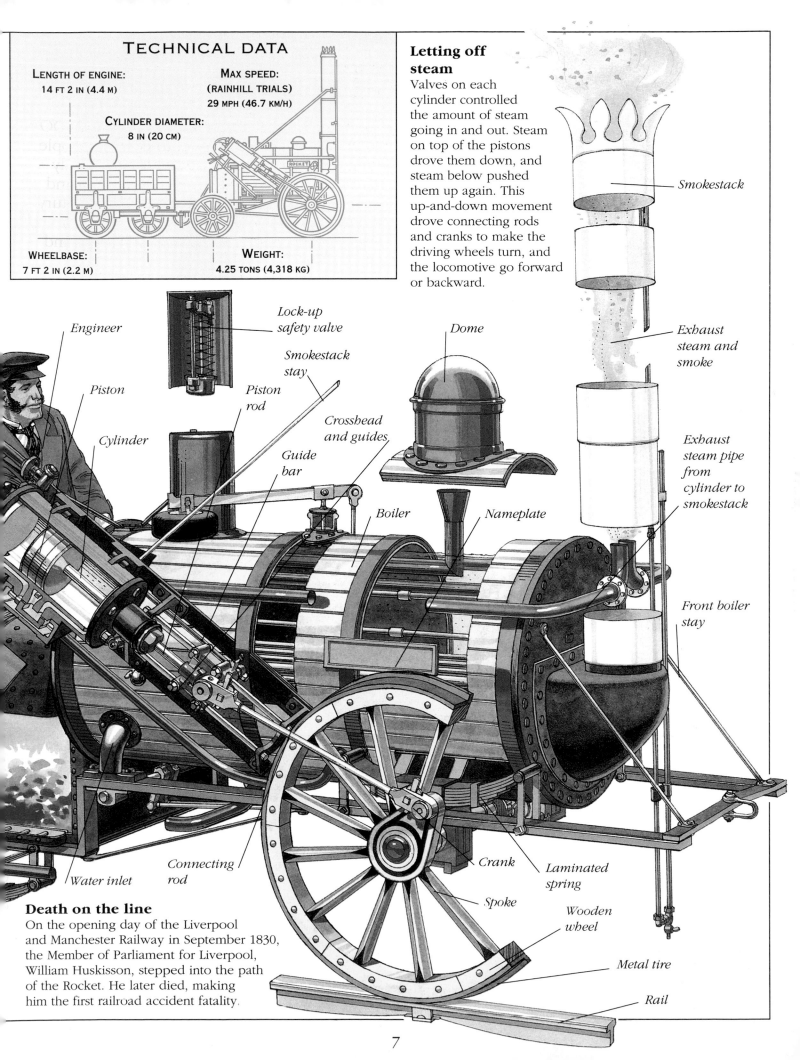

LENGTH OF ENGINE:
14 FT 2 IN (4.4 M)

MAX SPEED:
(RAINHILL TRIALS)
29 MPH (46.7 KM/H)

CYLINDER DIAMETER:
8 IN (20 CM)

WHEELBASE:
7 FT 2 IN (2.2 M)

WEIGHT:
4.25 TONS (4,318 KG)

Letting off steam

Valves on each cylinder controlled the amount of steam going in and out. Steam on top of the pistons drove them down, and steam below pushed them up again. This up-and-down movement drove connecting rods and cranks to make the driving wheels turn, and the locomotive go forward or backward.

Smokestack

Exhaust steam and smoke

Exhaust steam pipe from cylinder to smokestack

Front boiler stay

Engineer

Lock-up safety valve

Smokestack stay

Dome

Piston

Piston rod

Cylinder

Crosshead and guides

Guide bar

Boiler

Nameplate

Water inlet

Connecting rod

Crank

Laminated spring

Spoke

Wooden wheel

Metal tire

Rail

Death on the line

On the opening day of the Liverpool and Manchester Railway in September 1830, the Member of Parliament for Liverpool, William Huskisson, stepped into the path of the Rocket. He later died, making him the first railroad accident fatality.

CRAMPTON

CRAMPTON LOCOMOTIVES ARE NAMED AFTER THE MAN WHO designed them, Thomas Crampton (1816-88). In 1842, Crampton went to Belgium and began work on the locomotives that bear his name – engines with great driving wheels set behind the firebox. Seven years later, the Crampton No. 122, built by the French company J. F. Caile, made the first express journey between Paris and Calais in five hours. When England's Queen Victoria made a visit to France in 1855, it was a Crampton that was chosen to pull the royal train. In all, 320 engines were built to this design, most for use in France and Germany.

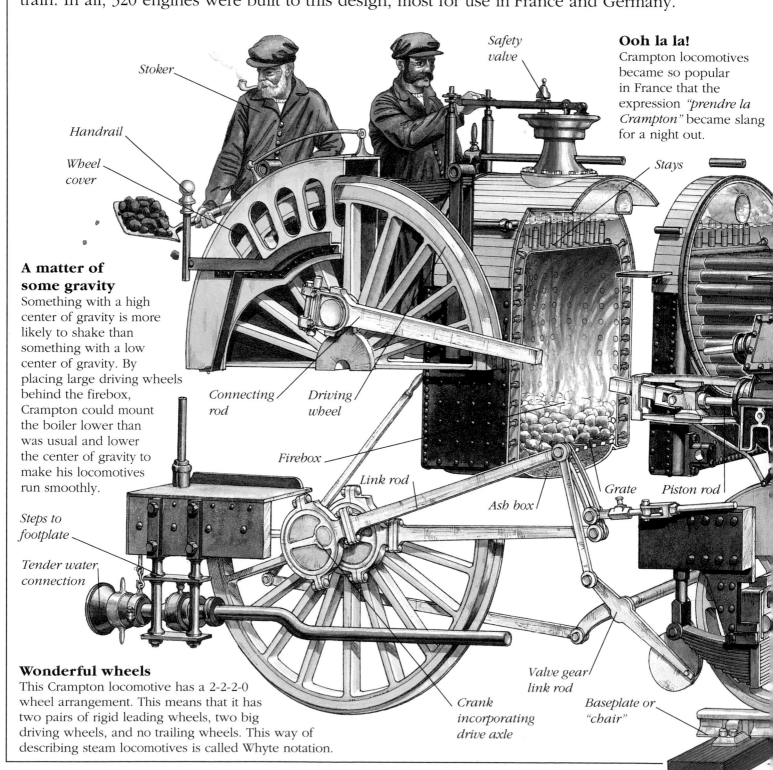

A matter of some gravity
Something with a high center of gravity is more likely to shake than something with a low center of gravity. By placing large driving wheels behind the firebox, Crampton could mount the boiler lower than was usual and lower the center of gravity to make his locomotives run smoothly.

Ooh la la!
Crampton locomotives became so popular in France that the expression *"prendre la Crampton"* became slang for a night out.

Wonderful wheels
This Crampton locomotive has a 2-2-2-0 wheel arrangement. This means that it has two pairs of rigid leading wheels, two big driving wheels, and no trailing wheels. This way of describing steam locomotives is called Whyte notation.

Stoker

Handrail

Wheel cover

Safety valve

Stays

Connecting rod

Driving wheel

Firebox

Link rod

Ash box

Grate

Piston rod

Steps to footplate

Tender water connection

Crank incorporating drive axle

Valve gear link rod

Baseplate or "chair"

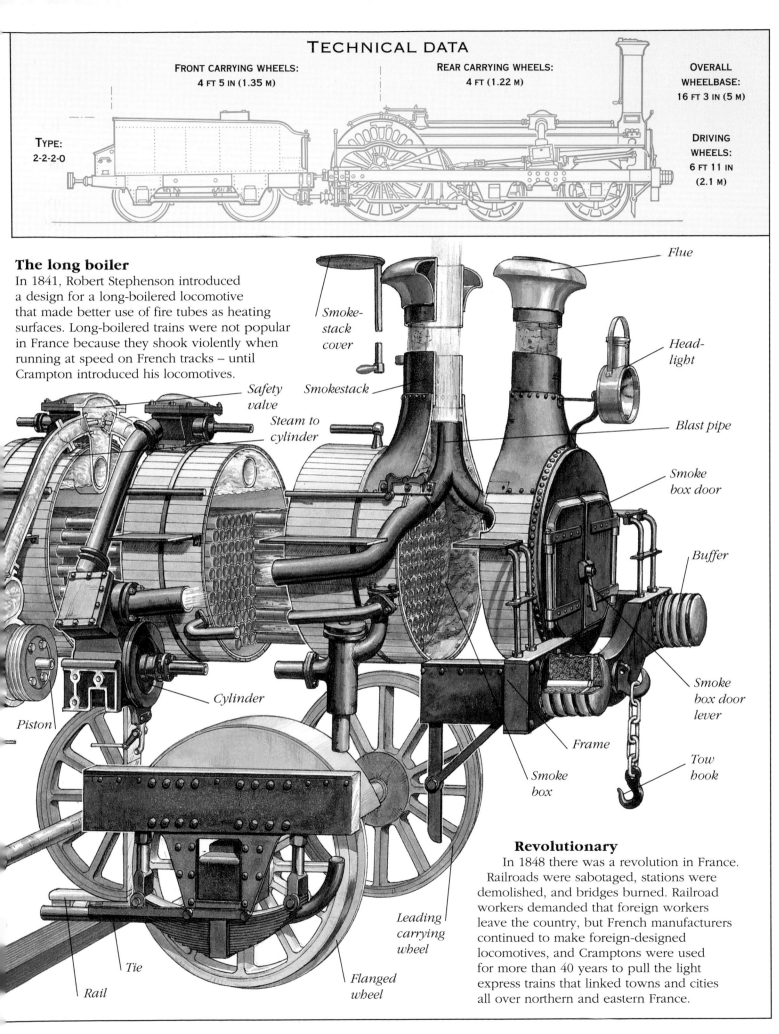

TECHNICAL DATA

| FRONT CARRYING WHEELS:
4 FT 5 IN (1.35 M) | REAR CARRYING WHEELS:
4 FT (1.22 M) | OVERALL
WHEELBASE:
16 FT 3 IN (5 M) |

TYPE:
2-2-2-0

DRIVING
WHEELS:
6 FT 11 IN
(2.1 M)

The long boiler

In 1841, Robert Stephenson introduced
a design for a long-boilered locomotive
that made better use of fire tubes as heating
surfaces. Long-boilered trains were not popular
in France because they shook violently when
running at speed on French tracks – until
Crampton introduced his locomotives.

Flue

*Smoke-
stack
cover*

Smokestack

*Safety
valve*

*Steam to
cylinder*

*Head-
light*

Blast pipe

*Smoke
box door*

Buffer

*Smoke
box door
lever*

Cylinder

Piston

Frame

*Tow
hook*

*Smoke
box*

*Leading
carrying
wheel*

Tie

Rail

*Flanged
wheel*

Revolutionary

In 1848 there was a revolution in France.
Railroads were sabotaged, stations were
demolished, and bridges burned. Railroad
workers demanded that foreign workers
leave the country, but French manufacturers
continued to make foreign-designed
locomotives, and Cramptons were used
for more than 40 years to pull the light
express trains that linked towns and cities
all over northern and eastern France.

AMERICAN 4-4-0

THE RAILROAD WAS VITAL IN OPENING UP THE VAST NORTH American continent, and one train more than any other became the workhorse of early American railroad development – the 4-4-0.

By 1870, about 85% of all locomotives in the US were 4-4-0s. Most had a distinctive balloon smokestack, designed to catch sparks from the wood fuel they burned. 4-4-0s were built in other countries, but they were so identified with the US that wherever they were built, they were usually called "Americans."

Light years ahead

There were few fenced-off tracks on US railroads, even when they ran through large-sized towns. Locomotive manufacturers were quick to fix a massive headlight to the front of each locomotive to warn people that a train was coming.

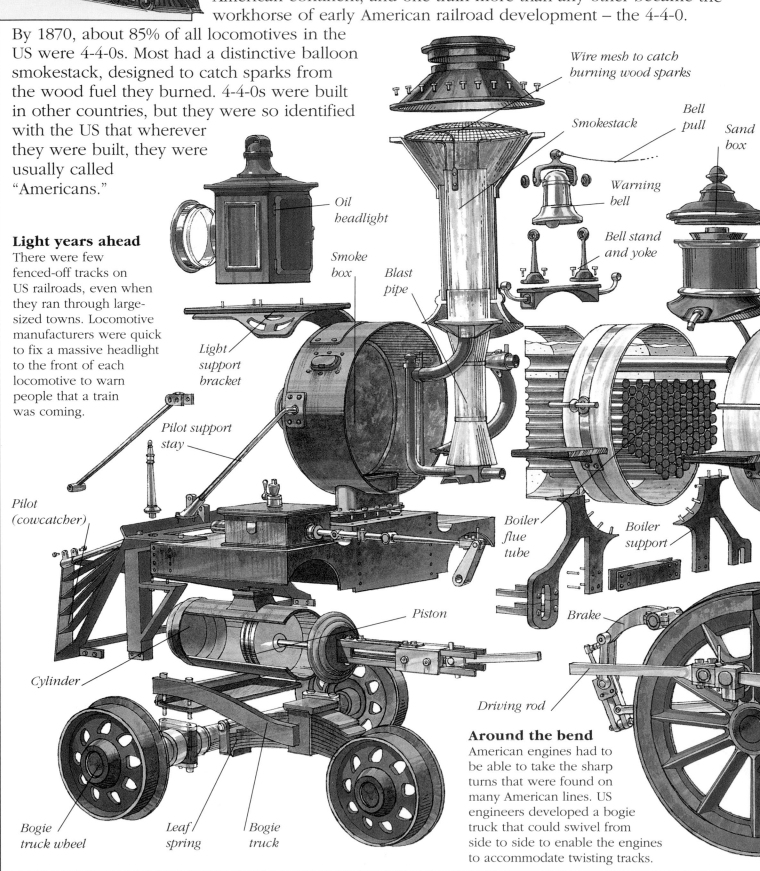

Wire mesh to catch burning wood sparks

Smokestack

Bell pull

Sand box

Oil headlight

Warning bell

Smoke box

Blast pipe

Bell stand and yoke

Light support bracket

Pilot support stay

Boiler flue tube

Boiler support

Pilot (cowcatcher)

Piston

Brake

Cylinder

Driving rod

Bogie truck wheel

Leaf spring

Bogie truck

Around the bend

American engines had to be able to take the sharp turns that were found on many American lines. US engineers developed a bogie truck that could swivel from side to side to enable the engines to accommodate twisting tracks.

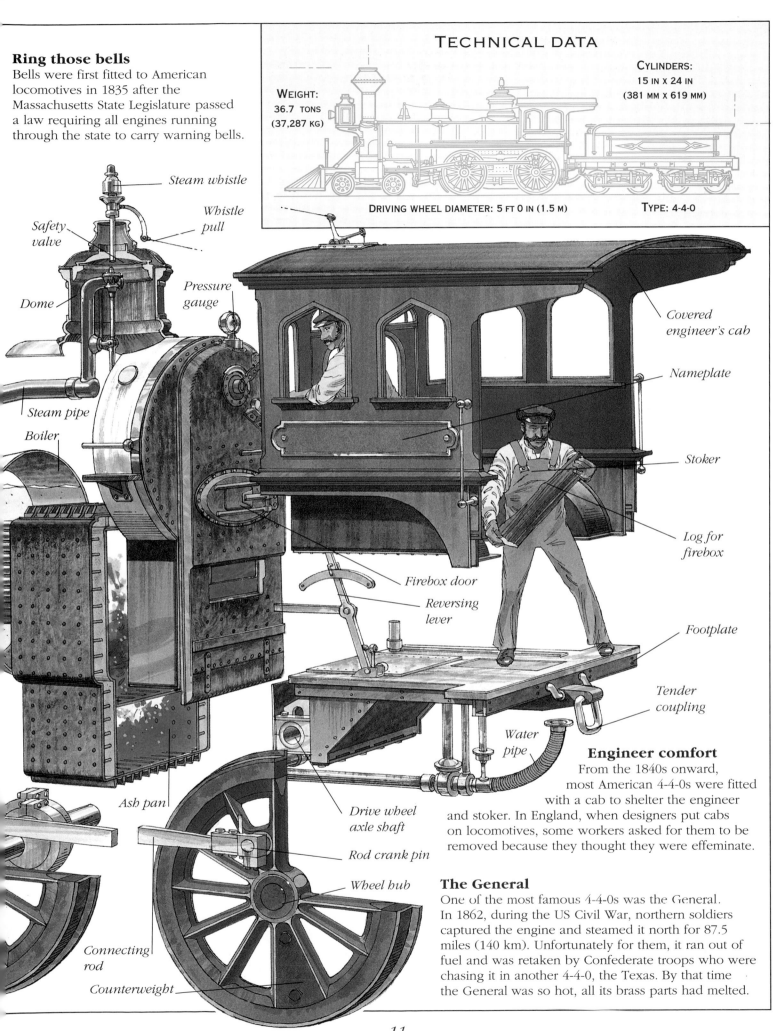

Ring those bells
Bells were first fitted to American locomotives in 1835 after the Massachusetts State Legislature passed a law requiring all engines running through the state to carry warning bells.

TECHNICAL DATA

WEIGHT:
36.7 TONS
(37,287 KG)

CYLINDERS:
15 IN X 24 IN
(381 MM X 619 MM)

DRIVING WHEEL DIAMETER: 5 FT 0 IN (1.5 M)

TYPE: 4-4-0

Steam whistle

Whistle pull

Safety valve

Dome

Pressure gauge

Steam pipe

Boiler

Covered engineer's cab

Nameplate

Stoker

Log for firebox

Firebox door

Reversing lever

Footplate

Tender coupling

Water pipe

Ash pan

Drive wheel axle shaft

Rod crank pin

Wheel hub

Connecting rod

Counterweight

Engineer comfort
From the 1840s onward, most American 4-4-0s were fitted with a cab to shelter the engineer and stoker. In England, when designers put cabs on locomotives, some workers asked for them to be removed because they thought they were effeminate.

The General
One of the most famous 4-4-0s was the General. In 1862, during the US Civil War, northern soldiers captured the engine and steamed it north for 87.5 miles (140 km). Unfortunately for them, it ran out of fuel and was retaken by Confederate troops who were chasing it in another 4-4-0, the Texas. By that time the General was so hot, all its brass parts had melted.

STIRLING "SINGLE"

THIS LOCOMOTIVE WAS DESIGNED BY PATRICK STIRLING, the chief designer of England's Great Northern Railway. It first shunted out of the company's Doncaster factory in 1870. Between then and 1893, when the last Stirling went into service, 47 were built, the most famous of them being Number 1. Its elegant lines, gleaming paintwork, and polished brass trim combined to make it one of the most beautiful engines ever. The most noticeable characteristic of these locomotives was the huge 8-ft (2.4-m) driving wheels, which allowed the engines to reach very high speeds.

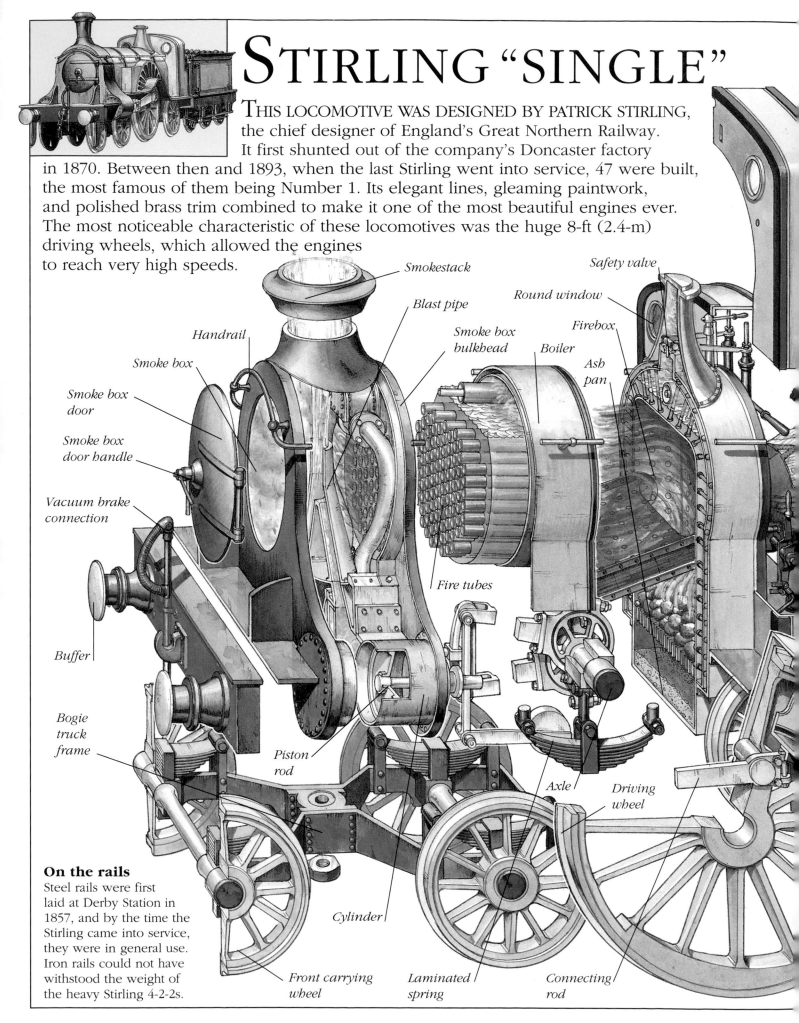

Smokestack

Blast pipe

Safety valve

Round window

Smoke box bulkhead

Firebox

Boiler

Ash pan

Handrail

Smoke box

Smoke box door

Smoke box door handle

Vacuum brake connection

Fire tubes

Buffer

Bogie truck frame

Piston rod

Axle

Driving wheel

On the rails

Steel rails were first laid at Derby Station in 1857, and by the time the Stirling came into service, they were in general use. Iron rails could not have withstood the weight of the heavy Stirling 4-2-2s.

Front carrying wheel

Cylinder

Laminated spring

Connecting rod

TECHNICAL DATA

OVERALL LENGTH (ENGINE):	WIDTH:
28 FT 11 IN (8.8 M)	7 FT 5 IN (2.26 M)

CYLINDER DIAMETER:	DRIVING WHEEL DIAMETER:	TYPE:
18 IN (457 MM)	8 FT 1 IN (2.4 M)	4-2-2

Clerestory

Luggage rack

Changes in appearance

The appearance of the Stirling changed slightly as more were built over the years. The splash guards on the first models were attractively slotted: later Stirlings had them closed in.

Coal bunker

Tender (section)

Coupling link

Coupling hook

Passenger compartment

Flange

Splash guard

Brake gear rod

Brake shoe

Slowing down

When the Stirling's driver pulled the brake lever, a vacuum was created in the brake pipe. This pushed the brake shoes onto the wheels and brought the train to a halt.

Laminated spring

A matter of some convenience

Until 1882, when passengers boarded a train, they had to stay in the same compartment until the train stopped – there was no way to move from one compartment to another. In that year, cars with a side aisle came into service. At each end of the aisle was a restroom – one for ladies only, the other strictly for gentlemen.

TANK ENGINE

AS RAILROADS DEVELOPED, SOME LOCOMOTIVE manufacturers recognized a need for an engine specially designed for short journeys and for pulling light trains.

These were the first tank engines, locomotives that carried their coal supply and water tanks on board the engine. Tank engines were more popular in England and the British Empire than in other parts of the world. The splendid tank engine shown here pulled trains in India.

Water on the side

Most tank engines carried their water in tanks set either in the sides of the engine or across on top. Because these latter ones looked a bit like saddle bags, they were called saddle tanks.

Giant tanks

Large tank engines first appeared in 1907 when England's Great Central Railway introduced a three-cylinder 0-8-4. It was used for shunting freight cars.

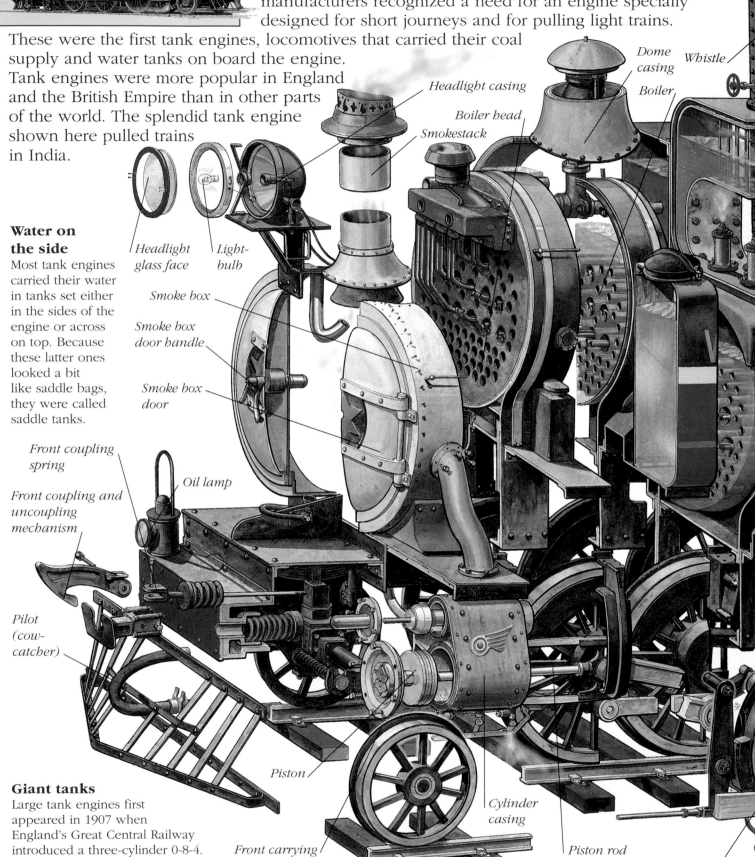

Headlight casing

Boiler head

Smokestack

Dome casing

Whistle

Boiler

Headlight glass face

Light-bulb

Smoke box

Smoke box door handle

Smoke box door

Front coupling spring

Front coupling and uncoupling mechanism

Oil lamp

Pilot (cow-catcher)

Piston

Front carrying wheel flange

Cylinder casing

Piston rod

Driving rod

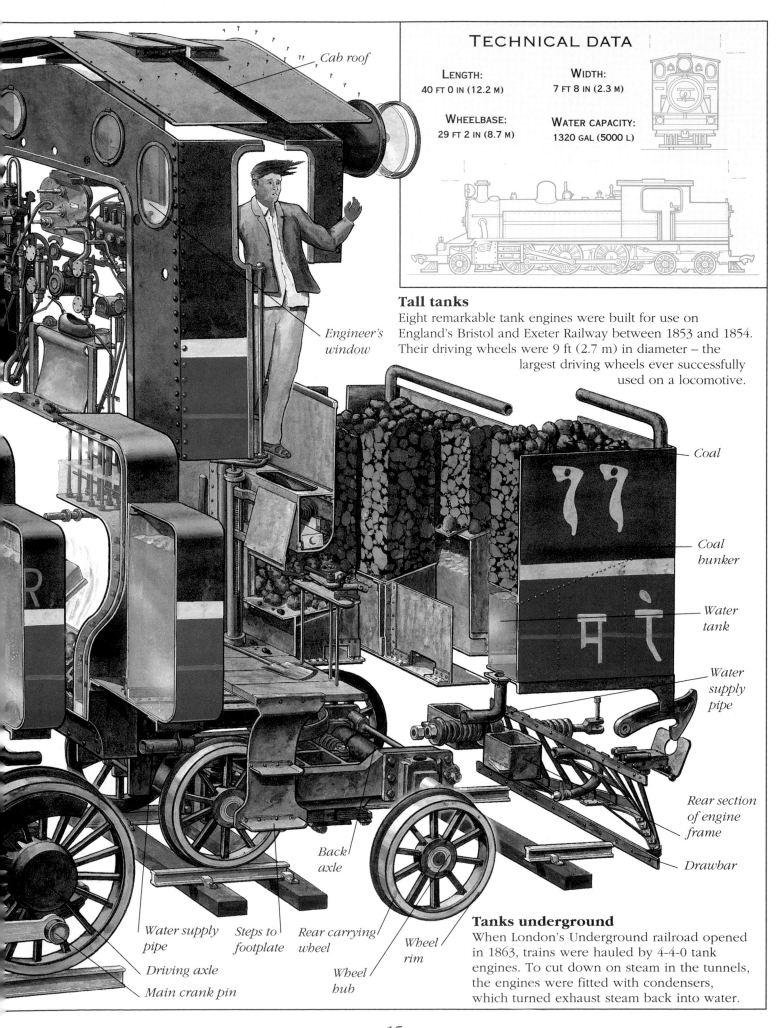

Cab roof

TECHNICAL DATA

LENGTH:
40 FT 0 IN (12.2 M)

WIDTH:
7 FT 8 IN (2.3 M)

WHEELBASE:
29 FT 2 IN (8.7 M)

WATER CAPACITY:
1320 GAL (5000 L)

Engineer's window

Tall tanks

Eight remarkable tank engines were built for use on England's Bristol and Exeter Railway between 1853 and 1854. Their driving wheels were 9 ft (2.7 m) in diameter – the largest driving wheels ever successfully used on a locomotive.

Coal

Coal bunker

Water tank

Water supply pipe

Rear section of engine frame

Drawbar

Water supply pipe

Steps to footplate

Rear carrying wheel

Wheel rim

Back axle

Driving axle

Wheel hub

Main crank pin

Tanks underground

When London's Underground railroad opened in 1863, trains were hauled by 4-4-0 tank engines. To cut down on steam in the tunnels, the engines were fitted with condensers, which turned exhaust steam back into water.

HEAVY FREIGHT

THE UNITED STATES IS A BIG COUNTRY WHERE BIG engines have to haul heavy freight and passenger trains over long distances. To do this, the Union Pacific Railroad introduced the remarkable 4-12-2 class in 1926. 4-12-2s had 12 driving wheels like the earlier Pennsylvania, an 0-12-0 built in 1863; and although 4-12-2s have long since run out of steam, they stand in the record books as the largest three-cylinder non-articulated engines ever built. The first of the class, Engine 9000, has been lovingly preserved by the southern California chapter of the Railway and Locomotive Historical Society for Preservation.

Great gear

Valve gears are required to coordinate the movement of the valves that allow steam into the cylinders with that of the pistons. The 4-12-2 was fitted with the British-developed Holcroft/Gresley combination gear to drive the valves of the middle cylinder.

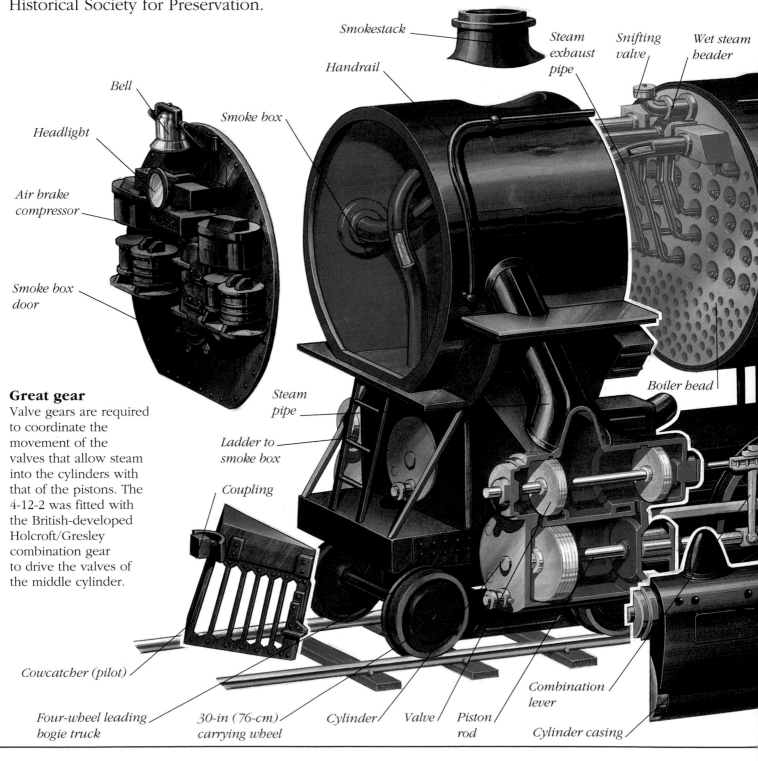

Smokestack

Handrail

Smoke box

Bell

Headlight

Air brake compressor

Smoke box door

Steam exhaust pipe

Snifting valve

Wet steam header

Boiler head

Steam pipe

Ladder to smoke box

Coupling

Cowcatcher (pilot)

Four-wheel leading bogie truck

30-in (76-cm) carrying wheel

Cylinder

Valve

Piston rod

Combination lever

Cylinder casing

Birth of a giant

After a series of test runs, Union Pacific decided that it wanted a non-articulated engine that married pulling power and speed. More tests led to a three-cylinder engine with four leading carrying wheels and two trailing carrying wheels – the 4-12-2.

On trial

The first 4-12-2 – the 9000 – was tested on a length of track that ran over a steep gradient. When its performance was compared with that of an articulated 2-8-8-0, the non-articulated engine was found to run faster on less fuel.

Steam dome

Sandbox

Sand pipe

Main steam valve

Superheater flue

Boiler wrapper

Fire tubes

Boiler feedwater heater

Crosshead

Eccentric rod

Coupling rod

Crank

Union link

Connecting rod

The biggest

The 4-12-2 was not the largest steam engine ever built. That record goes to another Union Pacific metal monster, the articulated Big Boy. An articulated locomotive has two independent sets of driving wheels separated by a pivot.

The brick arch

Like most steam locomotives, the 4-12-2 was fitted with an arch made of fireproof bricks at the front of the firebox. It acted as a baffle to make the coals burn at maximum heat and cut down the quantity of smoke produced.

Pressure gauge

Regulator handle

Pushing the coal in

The introduction of very large locomotives put heavy demands on the stokers who shoveled the coal. By 1913, many large tenders had steam coal pushers.

Engineer

Firebox support stays

Safety valve

Firebox crown sheet

Brick arch

Brake handle

Brake hose

Brake cylinder

Firebox

Ashpan

Running board

TRAILING BOGIE TRUCK

Going around the bend

The engineers who designed the 4-12-2 fitted a device to the front and rear driving wheels that allowed them to move laterally (from side to side). This, along with the two bogie trucks fitted with the carrying wheels, enabled the engine to go around bends that were as sharp as 16 degrees – and for a non-articulated engine, that was a very tight curve.

Trailing bogie truck axle

Bogie truck frame

Trailing bogie truck

45-in (114-cm) trailing carrying wheel

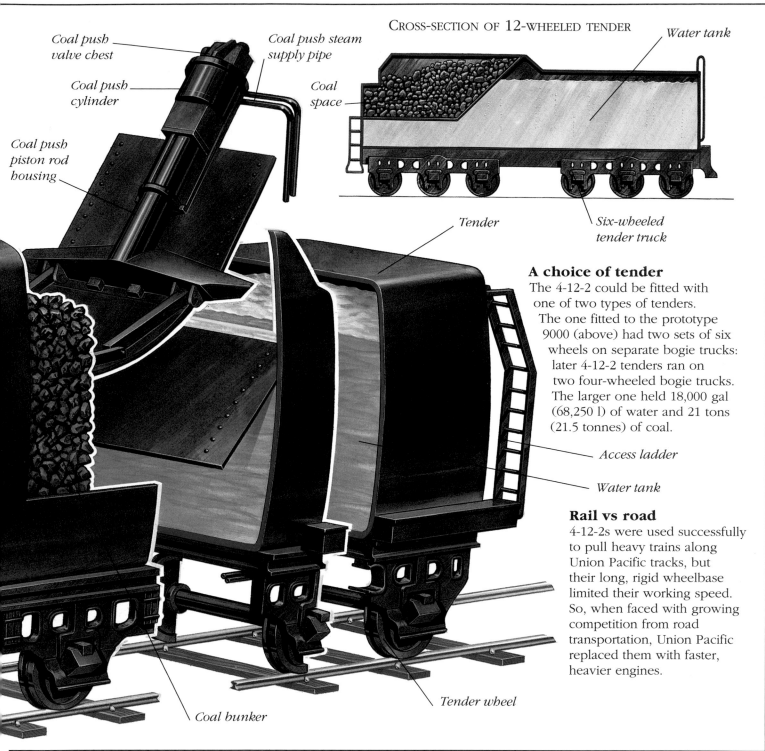

Coal push valve chest

Coal push cylinder

Coal push steam supply pipe

Coal push piston rod housing

Water tank

Coal space

Tender

Six-wheeled tender truck

A choice of tender

The 4-12-2 could be fitted with one of two types of tenders. The one fitted to the prototype 9000 (above) had two sets of six wheels on separate bogie trucks: later 4-12-2 tenders ran on two four-wheeled bogie trucks. The larger one held 18,000 gal (68,250 l) of water and 21 tons (21.5 tonnes) of coal.

Access ladder

Water tank

Rail vs road

4-12-2s were used successfully to pull heavy trains along Union Pacific tracks, but their long, rigid wheelbase limited their working speed. So, when faced with growing competition from road transportation, Union Pacific replaced them with faster, heavier engines.

Tender wheel

Coal bunker

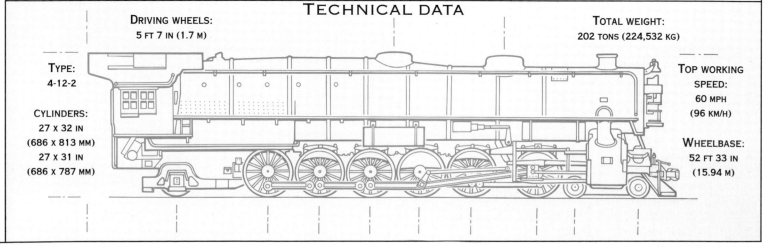

TECHNICAL DATA

DRIVING WHEELS:
5 FT 7 IN (1.7 M)

TOTAL WEIGHT:
202 TONS (224,532 KG)

TYPE:
4-12-2

TOP WORKING SPEED:
60 MPH
(96 KM/H)

CYLINDERS:
27 X 32 IN
(686 X 813 MM)
27 X 31 IN
(686 X 787 MM)

WHEELBASE:
52 FT 33 IN
(15.94 M)

PACIFIC

PACIFIC CLASS ENGINES take their name from the first 4-6-2 locomotive, built in America for the Missouri Pacific Railroad in 1902. Pacifics were introduced as a class in Britain in 1922 when Nigel Gresley's A1 Pacifics went into service for the Great Northern Railway (later the London and North-Eastern Railway) in 1922. The third A1 was one of the most famous engines ever – the Flying Scotsman.

Sir Nigel Gresley

Herbert Nigel Gresley was born in Edinburgh in 1876. In 1905 he was appointed Carriage and Wagon Superintendent of the Great Northern Railway. The A1, A3, and A4 Pacifics were famous engines he designed.

The Flying Scotsman

In 1862, the Great Northern Railway introduced a daily express to run the 393 miles (633 km) from London to Scotland. Within two years its reputation for speed was well established. A relief locomotive crew on board could run the Pacifics nonstop.

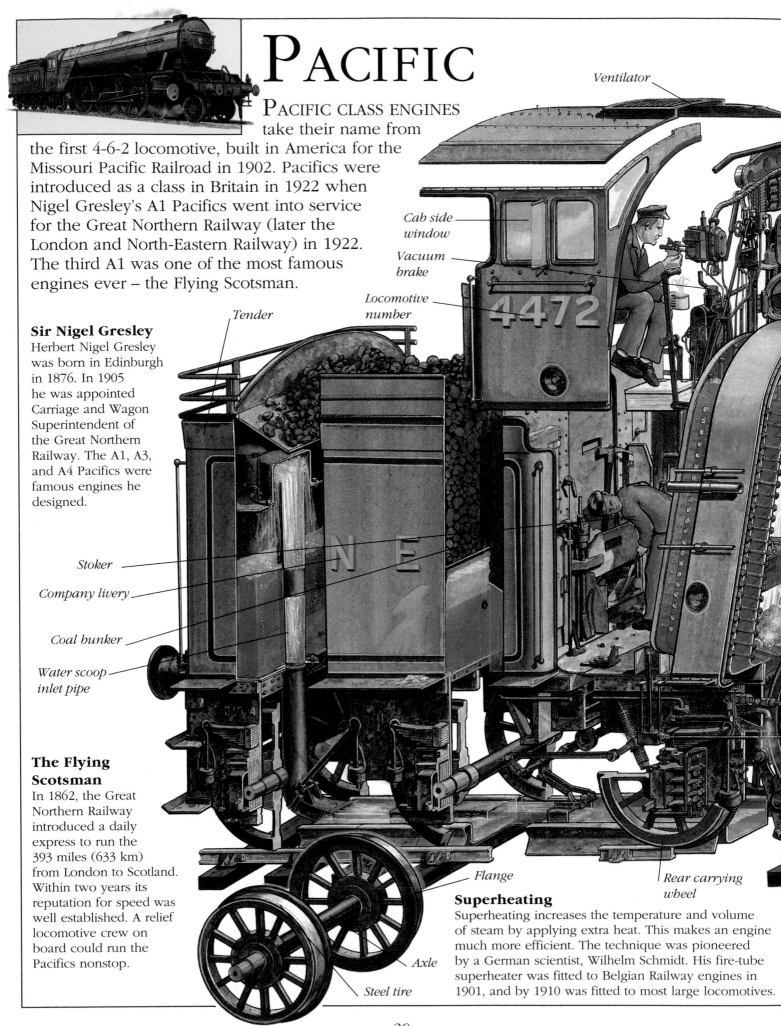

Ventilator

Cab side window

Vacuum brake

Locomotive number

Tender

Stoker

Company livery

Coal bunker

Water scoop inlet pipe

Flange

Rear carrying wheel

Axle

Steel tire

Superheating

Superheating increases the temperature and volume of steam by applying extra heat. This makes an engine much more efficient. The technique was pioneered by a German scientist, Wilhelm Schmidt. His fire-tube superheater was fitted to Belgian Railway engines in 1901, and by 1910 was fitted to most large locomotives.

TECHNICAL DATA

WEIGHT:
86.4 TONS
(87,782.4 KG)

OVERALL LENGTH:
70 FT 6 IN
(21.5 M)

DRIVING WHEELS: 6 FT 8 IN (2 M) DIAMETER

TYPE: 4-6-2

Firebox arch

Boiler tubes

Steam dome

Steam regulator valve

Smokestack

Blast pipe

Smoke box

Brake pipe connector

Light

FLYING SCOTSMAN

Main crank pin

Piston rod

Cylinder

Coupling rod

Front buffer

Cylinder valve

Piston

Working under pressure

A1 Pacifics had a boiler pressure of 180 lb/sq in. Shortly after they went to work, Gresley began experimenting with higher boiler pressures, and after a series of trials, a pressure of 220 lb/sq in was set as the standard for Pacific engines. The new series was designated A3 Pacific. In due course, as their boilers wore out, most A1 Pacifics were converted to A3s.

RACK LOCO

EARLY TRAINS COULD COPE WITH ONLY THE SLIGHTEST slopes, but in 1830 it was suggested that a locomotive could climb steep hills if it was fitted with a pair of wheels that would grip a rail laid in the middle of a standard railroad. The most common method of running a train up a hill became the rack railroad. The rack is the central rail, and it engages a pinion, a toothed wheel fitted to the underside of the engine.

Abt rack railroads

In 1882, Swiss railroad engineer Roman Abt patented his famous rack rail system. It eventually came to be used by more than 70% of all rack railroads. He used parallel toothed rails with the teeth of one rail opposite the gaps in the other, and a pair of pinions with teeth staggered to match.

Pushing from behind

Some mountain railroads have conventional track for part of the run and use rack and pinion for only the steepest gradients. In this case the locomotive works from the front of the train. But on railroads equipped with rack from end to end, the locomotive, with its brake system, is always placed at the downhill end of the train.

Cogged wheels

Pinion wheels have teeth all around their edges. As the wheels turn, the teeth slot into the gaps in the rack, literally climbing up it tooth by tooth, effectively pulling the engine up the slope and preventing it from slipping backward.

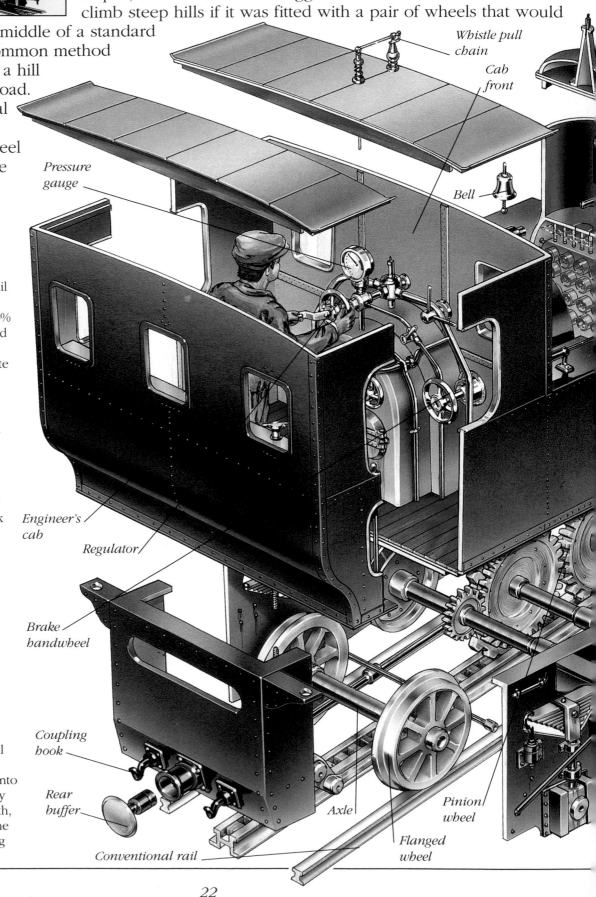

Whistle pull chain

Cab front

Pressure gauge

Bell

Engineer's cab

Regulator

Brake handwheel

Coupling hook

Rear buffer

Axle

Pinion wheel

Conventional rail

Flanged wheel

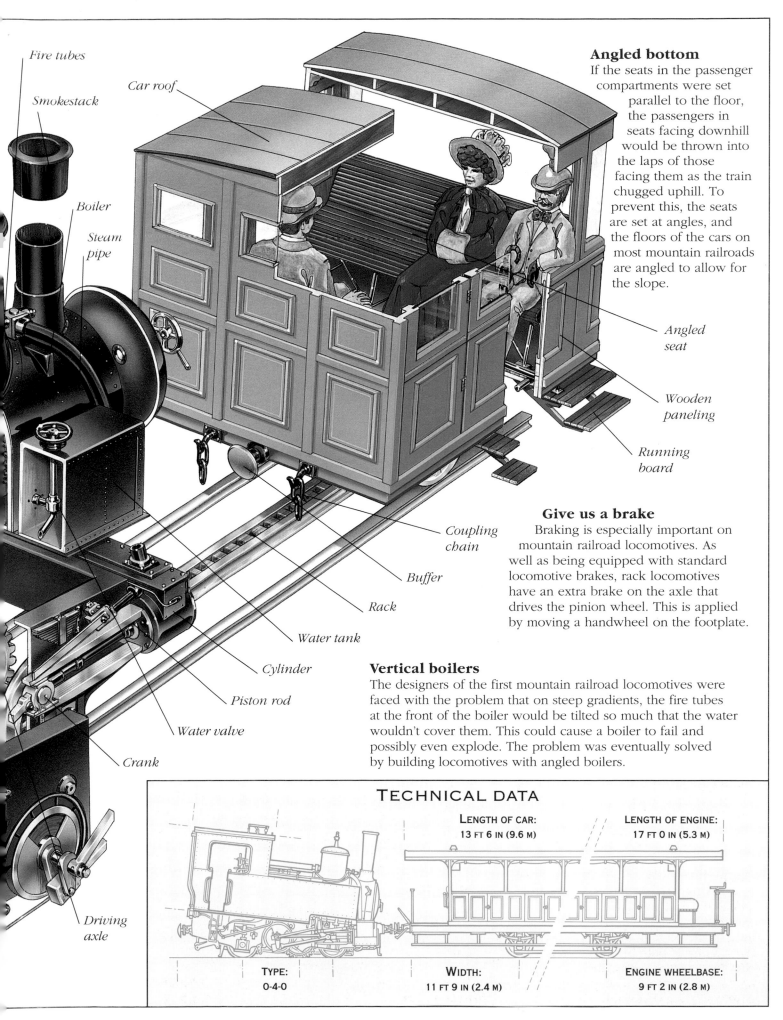

Fire tubes

Smokestack

Car roof

Boiler

Steam
pipe

Angled bottom
If the seats in the passenger
compartments were set
parallel to the floor,
the passengers in
seats facing downhill
would be thrown into
the laps of those
facing them as the train
chugged uphill. To
prevent this, the seats
are set at angles, and
the floors of the cars on
most mountain railroads
are angled to allow for
the slope.

Angled
seat

Wooden
paneling

Running
board

Coupling
chain

Buffer

Rack

Water tank

Cylinder

Piston rod

Water valve

Crank

Driving
axle

Give us a brake
Braking is especially important on
mountain railroad locomotives. As
well as being equipped with standard
locomotive brakes, rack locomotives
have an extra brake on the axle that
drives the pinion wheel. This is applied
by moving a handwheel on the footplate.

Vertical boilers
The designers of the first mountain railroad locomotives were
faced with the problem that on steep gradients, the fire tubes
at the front of the boiler would be tilted so much that the water
wouldn't cover them. This could cause a boiler to fail and
possibly even explode. The problem was eventually solved
by building locomotives with angled boilers.

TECHNICAL DATA

	LENGTH OF CAR: 13 FT 6 IN (9.6 M)	LENGTH OF ENGINE: 17 FT 0 IN (5.3 M)
TYPE: 0-4-0	WIDTH: 11 FT 9 IN (2.4 M)	ENGINE WHEELBASE: 9 FT 2 IN (2.8 M)

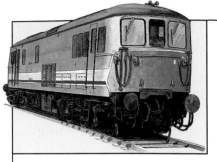

ELECTRO-DIESEL

ELECTRICITY WAS FIRST USED TO POWER A TRAIN IN 1842.
The first diesel locomotive engines ran 70 years later. Both
are more efficient than steam. The class 73 electro-diesel
shown here first ran for British Railways in 1962.

Diesels and electrics

Diesel locomotives use diesel engines to turn the wheels.
Electric trains run on electricity picked up from an
overhead wire or third rail. Diesel-electric trains use
diesel engines to generate electricity. This powers
the motors that turn the wheels. This class 73 uses
external electricity where available, but generates
its own where there is no third rail.

*Route
indicator*

*Windshield
wipers*

Engineer

Headlight

*Brake control
reservoirs*

Yellow at
both ends

Class 73s are painted
yellow at both ends to
make them more conspicious
to people working on the track.

*Cab
telephone
radio set*

*Cab
telephone
speaker*

CAB TELEPHONE
RADIO HANDSET

*Electric traction
control frame*

*Bogie truck
damper*

Axle box

*Hand brake
wheel*

Keeping in touch

Intercom sets are standard equipment
on class 73s. They allow the engineer
and other onboard crew members to
talk to each other throughout a journey.

Quick change

Where electricity is supplied by live
third rail, it flows to a transformer
where it is converted to the required
voltage for use in the locomotive.
The current then flows to traction
motors that turn the wheels.

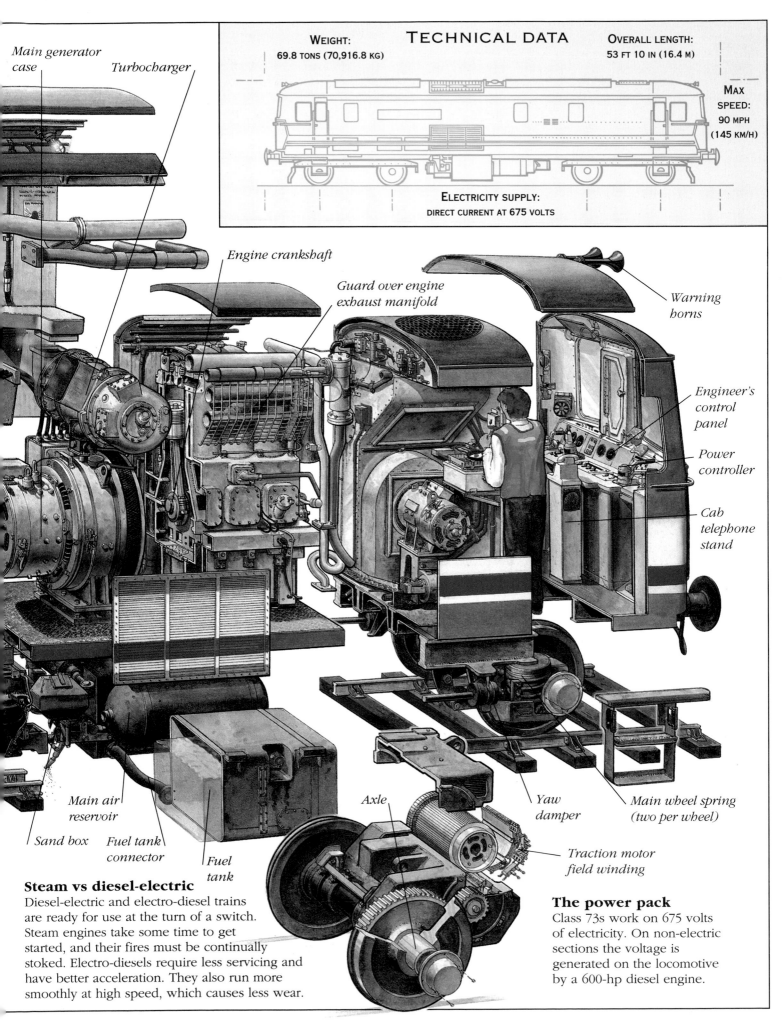

Main generator case

Turbocharger

TECHNICAL DATA

WEIGHT:
69.8 TONS (70,916.8 KG)

OVERALL LENGTH:
53 FT 10 IN (16.4 M)

MAX SPEED:
90 MPH (145 KM/H)

ELECTRICITY SUPPLY:
DIRECT CURRENT AT 675 VOLTS

Engine crankshaft

Guard over engine exhaust manifold

Warning horns

Engineer's control panel

Power controller

Cab telephone stand

Main air reservoir

Sand box

Fuel tank connector

Fuel tank

Axle

Yaw damper

Main wheel spring (two per wheel)

Traction motor field winding

Steam vs diesel-electric

Diesel-electric and electro-diesel trains are ready for use at the turn of a switch. Steam engines take some time to get started, and their fires must be continually stoked. Electro-diesels require less servicing and have better acceleration. They also run more smoothly at high speed, which causes less wear.

The power pack

Class 73s work on 675 volts of electricity. On non-electric sections the voltage is generated on the locomotive by a 600-hp diesel engine.

LE SHUTTLE

IN 1994 THE CHANNEL TUNNEL OPENED BETWEEN FOLKESTONE, in the south of England, and Calais, in northern France. From the start, British and French engineers realized that a new engine was needed to pull the trains that carry automobiles through the tunnel. The locomotive that came off the drawing board has to make the journey between France and England 20 times a day, so it is appropriately called Le Shuttle.

The controls
The driver has four main controls. The selector determines direction, either backward or forward. The power controller is pushed forward to accelerate the train. The main brake controller and direct-air brake controllers stop the train.

Power
Le Shuttle collects power from an overhead wire. The current is carried first to a small transformer, then to the main transformer. The current eventually reaches the traction motors that turn the wheels.

Overhead contact wire

Metallized carbon strip

Pantograph raised

Pantograph springs

Roof structure

Signaling equipment cubicle

Windshield

Engineer's cab

Captain's desk

Engineer's control panel

Headlight

Heavy duty buffer

Main converter

Bogie truck frame

Wheels and axle

Leading bogie truck

Coming to a halt
Le Shuttle is equipped with a combined electric (regenerative) and mechanical braking system.

The cabs
Each Shuttle locomotive has two cabs, a large one at the front extending across the entire width of the engine, and a smaller, auxiliary cab at the back, mainly used for switching operations at low speed.

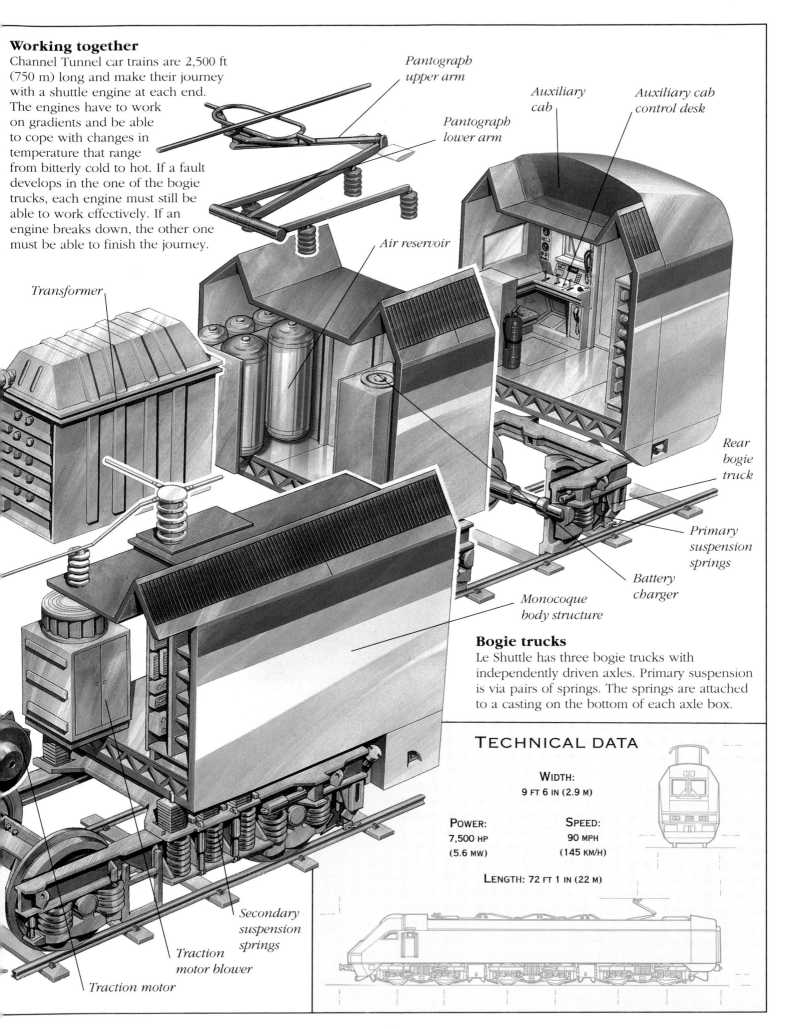

Working together

Channel Tunnel car trains are 2,500 ft (750 m) long and make their journey with a shuttle engine at each end. The engines have to work on gradients and be able to cope with changes in temperature that range from bitterly cold to hot. If a fault develops in the one of the bogie trucks, each engine must still be able to work effectively. If an engine breaks down, the other one must be able to finish the journey.

Pantograph upper arm

Pantograph lower arm

Auxiliary cab

Auxiliary cab control desk

Air reservoir

Transformer

Rear bogie truck

Primary suspension springs

Battery charger

Monocoque body structure

Bogie trucks

Le Shuttle has three bogie trucks with independently driven axles. Primary suspension is via pairs of springs. The springs are attached to a casting on the bottom of each axle box.

Secondary suspension springs

Traction motor blower

Traction motor

TECHNICAL DATA

WIDTH:
9 FT 6 IN (2.9 M)

POWER:
7,500 HP
(5.6 MW)

SPEED:
90 MPH
(145 KM/H)

LENGTH: 72 FT 1 IN (22 M)

TIMELINE

IN 1825, IT WAS NOT POSSIBLE TO travel more than a few miles by train. Within a few decades, railroad track had been laid all over the world. Today's advanced trains thunder along the tracks at speeds undreamed of by railroad pioneers.

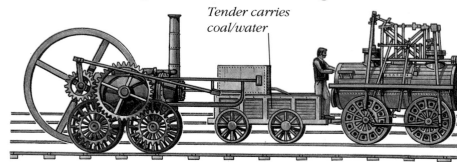

1803 Trevithick's locomotive England

1825 Locomotion England

Tender carries coal/water

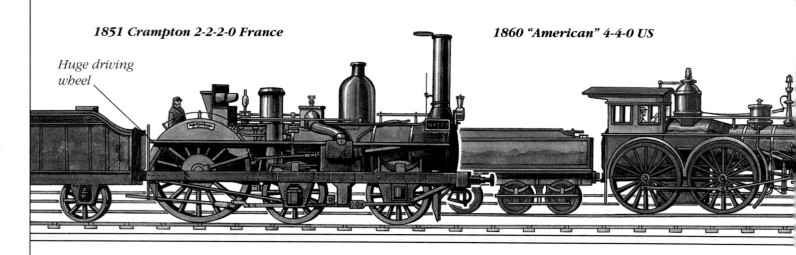

1851 Crampton 2-2-2-0 France

Huge driving wheel

1860 "American" 4-4-0 US

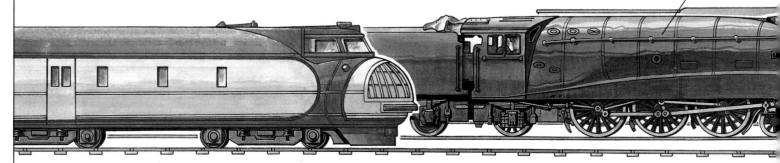

1934 M-10000 diesel unit US – one of the first diesel trains

**1938 Mallard 4-6-2 England
Steam speed record holder – 126 mph (202 km/h)**

Streamlined shape

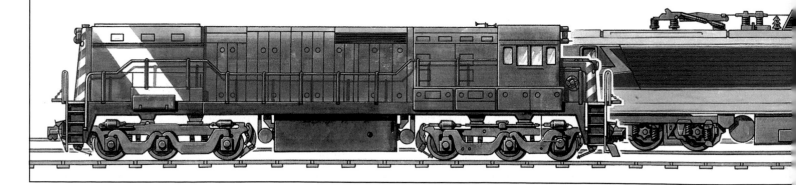

1955 General Electric diesel locomotive US

1970 Electric express locomotive France

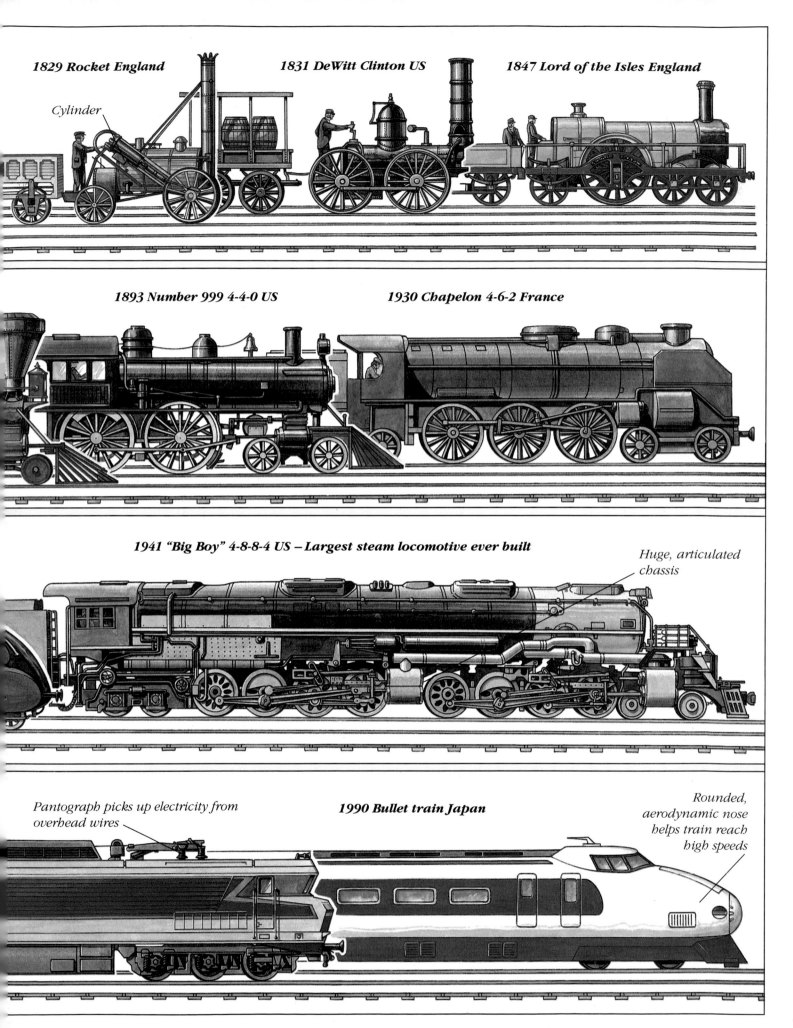

1829 Rocket England

Cylinder

1831 DeWitt Clinton US

1847 Lord of the Isles England

1893 Number 999 4-4-0 US

1930 Chapelon 4-6-2 France

1941 "Big Boy" 4-8-8-4 US – Largest steam locomotive ever built

Huge, articulated chassis

Pantograph picks up electricity from overhead wires

1990 Bullet train Japan

Rounded, aerodynamic nose helps train reach high speeds

GLOSSARY

Air brakes
A system that uses compressed air to push the brake shoes onto the wheels.

Axle
A round metal bar that joins a pair of wheels together.

Ballast
Small pebbles that make up the base of a railroad track.

Blast pipe
The pipe in a steam locomotive that takes exhaust steam up the smokestack.

Boiler
The metal drum in a steam locomotive where water is turned into steam.

Bogie truck
The wheeled carriage fitted beneath the end of a locomotive or car.

Bogie truck

Cab
The engineer's compartment – where the controls are located.

Car
A vehicle in which passengers travel. Passenger cars, or coaches, carry people. Freight cars carry all kinds of things from place to place.

Carrying wheel
A locomotive's guiding, load-bearing wheel.

Coal pusher
A steam-operated device in the tender for pushing coal forward to a point where it can be shoveled directly into the firebox.

Cog wheel
A toothed wheel or pinion that connects with the rack laid between the rails of a rack-and-pinion mountain railroad.

Collector shoe
The metal block that collects electric current from the live rail in third-rail electrified tracks.

Connecting rod
A metal rod that links the piston to the driving wheels of a locomotive.

Coupling
A device for connecting cars to an engine and each other.

Cowcatcher
A metal grid fitted to the front of a locomotive to nudge animals off the track (technically called the pilot).

Coupling rods
The metal rod that links one wheel of a pair to the other, so that they turn in unison.

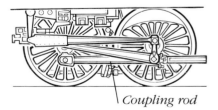
Coupling rod

Crankshaft
A metal arm that transfers the movement of a piston to the wheels, making them turn.

Crosshead
A device that keeps the piston rods in line as they move in and out of the cylinder.

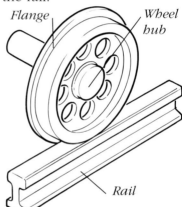
Crosshead

Cylinder
The metal tube into which steam or gas is pushed to make the pistons go backward and forward.

Dead-man's handle
A device for cutting off power and applying brakes in the event of the engineer becoming ill during a trip.

Diesel engine
An engine, fueled by diesel oil, used in some trains either to power the engine directly or to drive the electric motors that power the engine.

Dome
The part on top of the boiler barrel of a steam locomotive where dry steam is collected and where the steam regulator valve is set.

Driving wheels
The main wheel of a locomotive turned by the movement of the connecting rod.

Electro-diesel engine
An engine that can run on both electrified and non-electrified tracks.

Exhaust
The unwanted fumes that come from the boiler.

Firebox
The metal box situated behind the boiler of a steam locomotive in which the fire burns.

Fire stoker
The person who keeps the fire fueled in a steam locomotive.

Flange
The extended rim of a wheel that keeps it on the rail.

Flange   *Wheel hub*

Rail

Footplate
The part of a steam locomotive on which the engineer and stoker stand.

Frame
The foundation or chassis on which a steam locomotive is built.

Freight
The goods or cargo carried on a train.

Gauge
The distance between the two rails of a railroad track.

Gradient
The slope of a railroad track.

uard

he official in charge of
n English train.

and brake

he means of applying
ake blocks to the
heels without power
sistance.

ocomotive

n engine that makes
own power to enable
to move. Locomotives
ed to be powered
steam, but since
e 1930s, electricity
d diesel power have
ken over because
ey are cheaper
d more efficient.

ve rail

n electrical conductor for
ansmitting electricity to a
comotive on third-rail
ectrified tracks.

antograph

wire frame on top of
electric train that
cks up electricity
om cables suspended
ove the track.

ston

metal plug powered
steam that slides
rward and backward
side a cylinder.

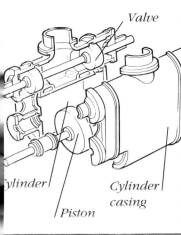

Valve

ylinder *Cylinder casing* *Piston*

Piston rod

The rod that connects the
piston to the crosshead.

Rack and pinion

The toothed track (rack)
and toothed wheel
(pinion) that pull trains
up and down steep
mountains and other
slopes.

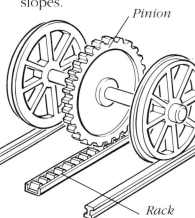

Pinion

Rack

Rail

The strip of steel on which
a train's wheels run.

Rail bed

The layer of material
spread over the formation
on which the ties and
track are laid. Also
called ballast bed.

Rolling stock

Cars, coaches, and other
railroad vehicles.

Safety valve

The apparatus inside
the dome of a steam
locomotive from which
steam is released if
pressure inside the
boiler becomes too
high.

Sandbox

A box in which sand is
stored to be fed by pipes
onto the rail ahead of the
driving wheels to stop
them from slipping.

Shoe brake

A device that stops a
turning wheel by pressing
a block of wood or metal
to the rim.

Shoe brake

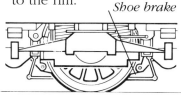

Shunting

Pushing cars and coaches
into the correct order to
form a train.

Signals

A means of
controlling the
movement of trains by
warning or advising the
engineer if there are trains
on the track ahead, or of
the intention to divert a
train to another track.

Smokestack

The metal tube from which
steam and smoke is
emitted.

Tie

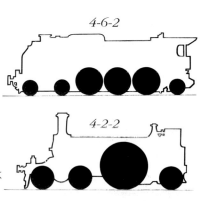

Smoke box

The compartment in a
steam locomotive where
steam and smoke collect
before being sent up the
smokestack.

Spark arrester

A device in the smokestack
to prevent sparks from
being thrown into the air.

Superheating

Increasing the temperature

and volume of steam in
a steam locomotive after
it has left the boiler barrel
by applying extra heat.

Suspension

The springed system
between the wheels
and frame that absorbs
shock caused by running
over uneven tracks.

Tank engine

An engine that carried
its own water and fuel
on its chassis rather than
in a separate tender. Tank
engines were usually used
for short runs with
lightweight trains.

Tender

A car, attached to a steam
locomotive, that carries the
locomotive's water and
fuel, either wood or coal.

Tie

The wooden or concrete
strip to which rails are
attached.

Wheel code (Whyte notation)

The classification of
steam engines by number
of wheels.

4-6-2

4-2-2

4-4-0

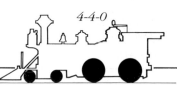

INDEX

A

Abt rack railroad, 22
Abt, Roman, 22
American 4-4-0, 10-11, 28
articulated locomotives, 16

B

bells, warning, 11
bogie trucks, 10, 18, 19, 26, 27
"Big Boy," 16, 29
boiler, 6, 8, 9, 23
boiler pressure, 21
brakes, 13, 22, 23, 26
brick arch, 18
Bristol and Exeter Railway, 15
British Railways class 73 electro-diesel, 24-25
Bullet train, 29

C

Caile, J.F., 8
chairs, 6
Channel Tunnel, 26
Chapelon 4-6-2, 29
coal, 6, 18, 19
coal push, 18, 30
connecting rod, 7
cab, 11, 30
Crampton 2-2-2-0, 8-9, 28
Crampton, Thomas, 8
cranks, 7
cylinder valves, 7, 17, 31
cylinders, 6, 7

D

DeWitt Clinton, 29

E

electric trains, 24, 26-27, 28
Engine 9000, 16

engines

diesel, 24, 28
diesel-electric, 24, 25
electric, 24, 26-27, 28
electro-diesel, 24-25
steam, 6-21, 25

F

firebox, 6, 8, 18, 30
fire tubes, 6, 9, 23
Flying Scotsman, 20-21

G

General, 11
Great Central Railway, 14
Great Northern Railway, 12, 20
Gresley, Sir Nigel, 20

H

headlights, 10
heavy freight locomotive, 16-19
Huskisson, William, 7

I

intercom, 24

L

Le Shuttle, 26-27
Liverpool and Manchester Railway, 6, 7
Locomotion, 28
locomotives see engines
London and North-Eastern Railway, 20
Lord of the Isles, 29

M

M-10000 diesel, 28
Mallard, 28

Missouri Pacific Railroad, 20
mountain railroads, 22-23

N

Number 999, 29

O

overhead wire, 26, 29

P

Pacific class A1, 20-21
Pacific class A3, 20-21
Pacific class A4, 20
pantograph, 29
Pennsylvania, 16
passenger compartments, 13, 23
pistons, 7, 31

R

rack and pinion, 22, 23
rack loco, 22-23
radio handset, 24
rails, 6, 12, 22, 25
Rocket, 6-7, 29

S

saddle tanks, 14
Schmidt, Wilhelm, 20
selector, 26
side aisle, 13
splash guards, 13
steam dome, 6
Stephenson, Robert, 6, 9
Stirling, Patrick, 12
Stirling "Single" no.1, 12-13
superheating, 20
suspension, 26

T

tank engines, 14-15
tenders, 18, 19, 31
Texas, 11

third (live) rail, 24, 25
traction motors, 24, 26
track, 8, 10, 19, 22, 28
transformer, 24, 26
Trevithick's locomotive, 28
types of locomotive
0-8-4, 14
0-12-0, 16
2-2-2-0, 8-9, 28
2-8-8-0, 17
4-2-2, 12-13
4-4-0, 10-11, 28, 29
4-6-2, 20-21, 28
4-12-2, 16-19

U

Union Pacific Railroad, 16, 17, 19
Union Pacific engine no. 9000, 16-17

V

valve gear, 17
valves, 31
steam, 7, 31

W

warning bells, 11
wheel code, 8, 31
wheels
carrying, 17, 18, 30
driving, 7, 8, 12, 15, 16, 18, 28, 30
pinion, 22, 31

Acknowledgments

Dorling Kindersley would like to thank the following people who helped in the preparation of this book:
Index by Lynn Bresler
Artworks by:
Alan Austin
Gary Biggin
Richard Chasemore
Hans Jenssen
Chris Lyon